T0197400

A *Year*
in
New England

A Nature Acrostic Poem Book about Months

DIANE L. TREICHLER

ILLUSTRATED BY RAYMOND F. TAMEO

AuthorHouse™
1663 Liberty Drive
Bloomington, IN 47403
www.authorhouse.com
Phone: 833-262-8899

Because of the dynamic nature of the Internet, any web addresses or links contained in
this book may have changed since publication and may no longer be valid. The views
expressed in this work are solely those of the author and do not necessarily reflect the
views of the publisher, and the publisher hereby disclaims any responsibility for them.

This book is printed on acid-free paper.

ISBN: 978-1-6655-3035-4 (sc)
ISBN: 978-1-6655-3036-1 (e)

Scripture taken from the Holy Bible, New International Version®. Copyright ©
1973, 1978, 1984 Biblica. Used by permission of Zondervan. All rights reserved.

Print information available on the last page.

Published by AuthorHouse 06/25/2021

authorHOUSE®

To Doug, Jenna, and Tyler - for experiencing
nature with me and loving me

To my parents, Dot and Ray - for teaching
me the love of the great outdoors

To my sister, Dawn - for the inspiration

To all my students - past, present, and future

John 1:3a NIV

Just enjoying the first snow

A path of footsteps

Newly painted ice on windows

Unbelievably cold air

Another gray sky

Red cardinal on birch tree

Year of new beginnings

Frosty days

Evergreens sway

Be my Valentine

Rich scent of pinecones

Unyielding windy days

A hope for spring

Radiant colorful sky

Yes, deep winter and hibernation

Muddy afternoons

A day for kite flying

Red barn afar

Chilly mornings

Hilltop of pussy willows

A new season

Perfect rainbows

Rainy days for spring blossoms

In the garden daffodils dancing towards the sun

Landscape of budding trees

Meandering beside a stone wall

A regal guest – a monarch butterfly

Yellow buds along a dirt path

Joyful blue skies and dunes

Under the rippling waves

Never enough ample sun

Eating anything strawberry

Jubilant booming fireworks

Under a blanket of stars

Long lazy summer days

Yard celebrations

An abundance of hot hazy days

Under the big blue sky

Getting to the lake and canoeing

Unwavering heatwaves

Swimming around the island

Tails - cat o' nine tails, that is

"Tameo's Island"

Shorter days

Eating up the harvest

Preparing for cool weather

That first crisp morning

Echoes of the crows

Migrating South

Beautiful walks in the woods

Enjoying apple orchards

Rising of a scarecrow

Oh - the harvest moon

Cool days carving pumpkins

The leaves of crimson, orange, and gold

Over the pumpkin vines

Being a leaf peeper

Essence of fall spices: nutmeg, cinnamon, cloves

Remember the squirrels hoarding acorns

Narrow rows of barren cornstalks

Observing nature

Visiting family and friends

Every one feasts

Many leaves fallen

Baking pies

Everything turkey

Remembering America's history

Dashing across the frozen ice

Ever the fireplace burns

Cozy homestead

Enjoying a recent snowfall

Mountains white-capped

Bushes of holly

Eagerly waiting Christmas

Red winterberry

Printed in the United States
by Baker & Taylor Publisher Services